T0351892

THE RAF
COLOURING BOOK

First published 2018

The History Press
The Mill, Brimscombe Port
Stroud, Gloucestershire, GL5 2QG
www.thehistorypress.co.uk

British Library Cataloguing in Publication Data.
A catalogue record for this book is available from the British Library.

ISBN 978 0 7509 8891 9

Typesetting and origination by The History Press
Printed in Turkey by Imak

THE RAF
COLOURING BOOK

The RAF was formed in 1918, as a merger of the Royal Naval Air Service and the Royal Flying Corps; it was the first independent air force in the world. Over the years many aircraft have come and gone, as the RAF continually adapts to the demands of warfare and peacekeeping across rapidly evolving theatres. The drawings in this book celebrate the diversity of aircraft, from biplanes to bombers, from jet to delta wing, through to the fighter, surveillance, air mobility aircraft and helicopters of today. Within these pages are arresting Second World War scenes that highlight the significance of the Battle of Britain and the Dams Raid, as well as the key figures of R.J. Mitchell and flying ace Douglas Bader. This book celebrates the might of the RAF across a century of patrolling the skies.

Sopwith Camel. ▸

N
F6034

De Havilland Tiger Moth. ▸

Supermarine S.6B racing seaplane,
winner of the 1931 Schneider Trophy,
with the RAF High Speed Flight. ▸

2

Gloster Gladiator I. ▸

Handley Page Halifax bomber. ▸

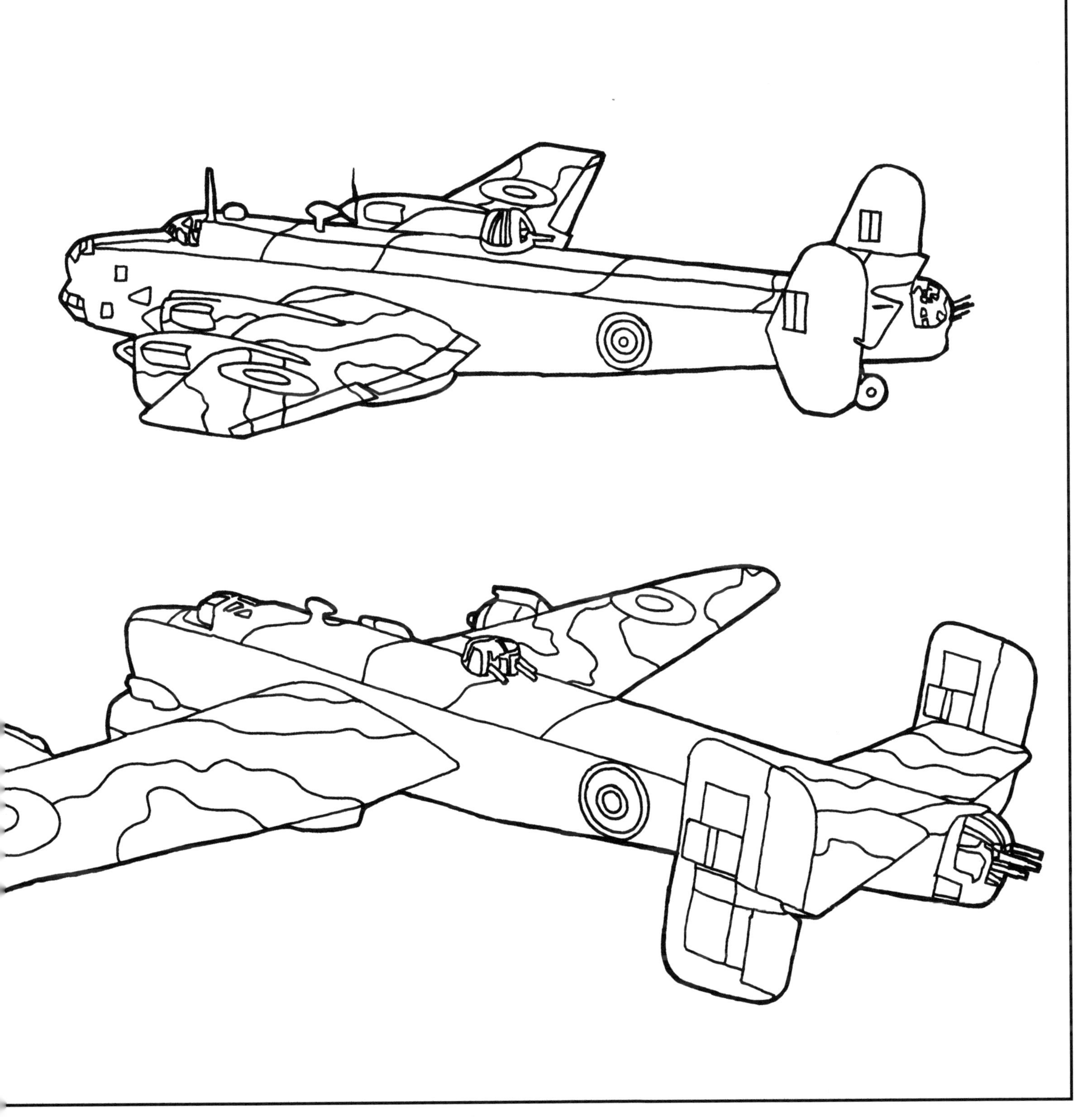

Hawker Fury. ▸

Gloster Gauntlet Mk I. ▸

The Battle of Britain in the summer of 1940: Heinkel HE 111s, Messerschmitt BF 109s and Hurricanes. ▸

Hurricane, Spitfire and
Lancaster: stalwarts of the skies. ▸

R.J. Mitchell and his most famous aircraft. ▸

Supermarine Spitfire. ▸

CR S

De Havilland DH.98 Mosquito B.XVI. ▸

Avro Anson C.19. ▸

The Battle of Britain rages on,
with Spitfires versus Stukas. ▸

S

Vickers Wellington bombers. ▸

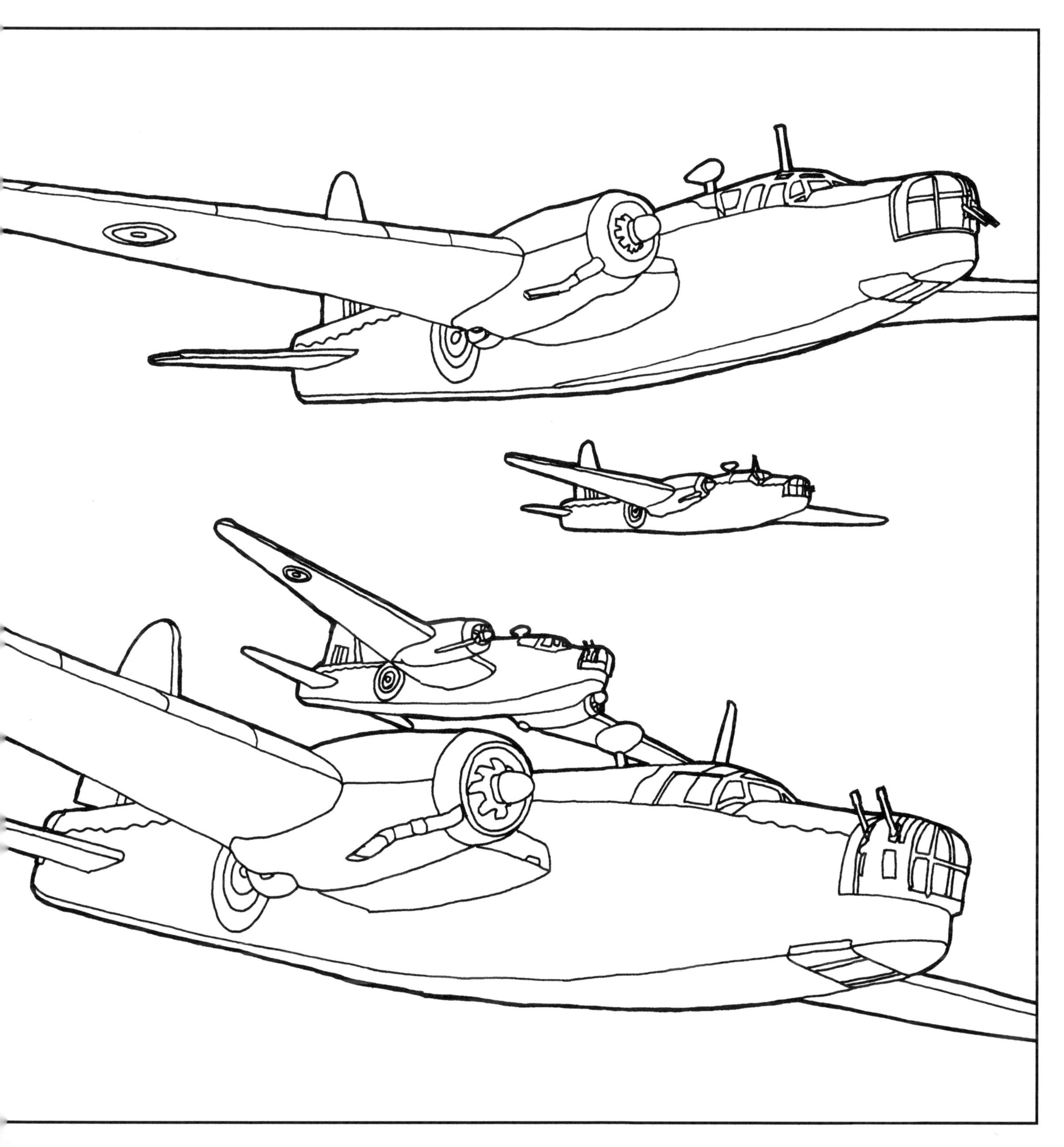

Avro Lancaster bomber. ▸

KCOA
VROA
KB726

Spitfire in flight. ▸

Hawker Hurricane, Mks I and II. ▸

Douglas Bader stands on
the wing of his Hurricane. ▸

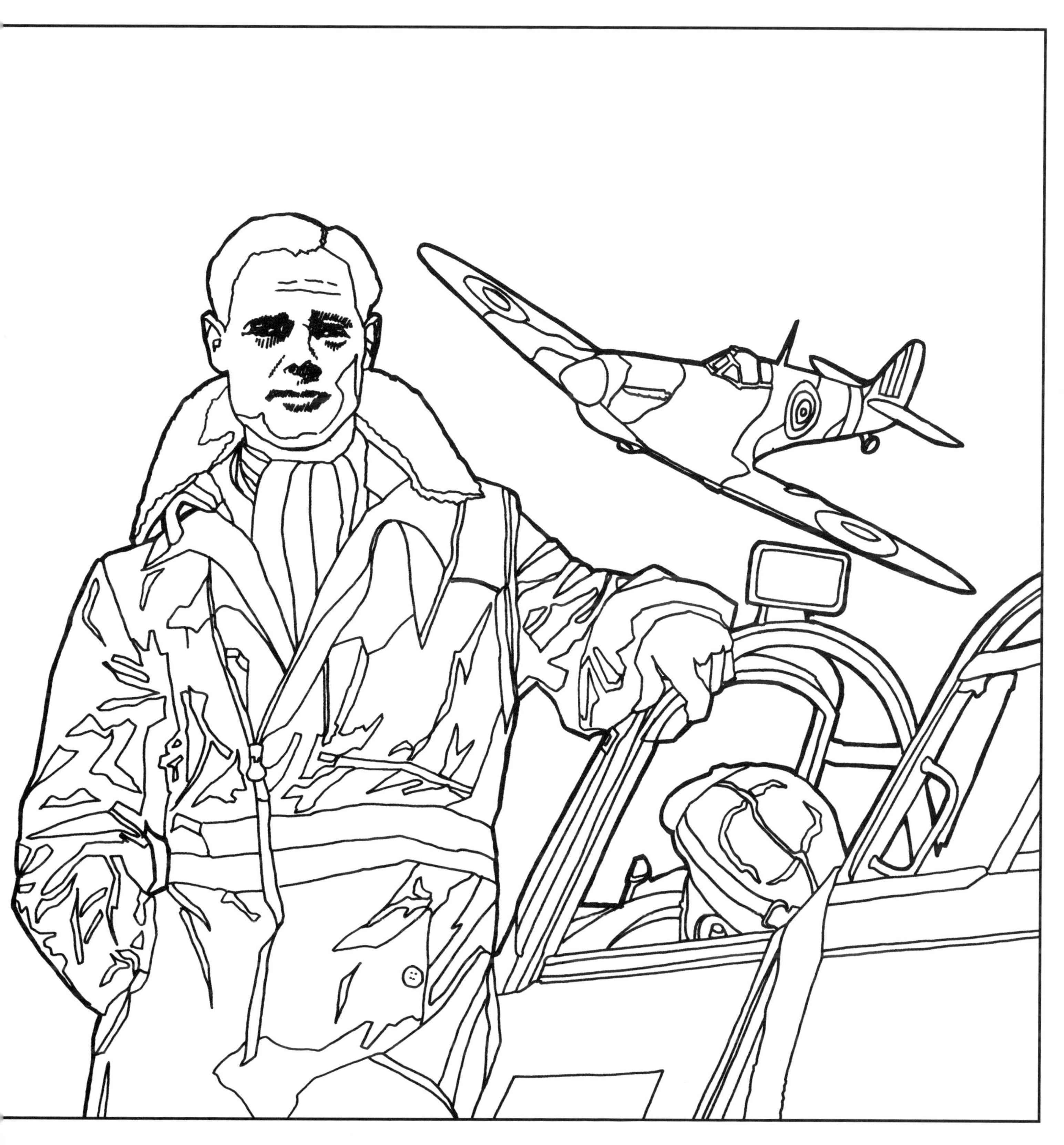

Westland Whirlwind I. ▸

Hawker Typhoon MK IB. ▸

Operation Chastise – The Dams Raid, 16–17 May 1943. ▸

The first British jet-engined aircraft to fly:
Gloster Whittle/Pioneer E28/39. ▸

Gloster Meteor, the first operational British jet fighter. ▸

De Havilland DH-106 Comet transporter. ▸

ROYAL AIR FORCE TRANSPORT COMMAND

English Electric Canberra PR7. ▸

Gloster Javelin FAW.1 and FAW.9 ▸

Avro Vulcan B Mk 2. ▸

English Electric/BAC Lightning F.6 and F.3. ▸

R

Hawker Hunter T7, with Gloster Meteor. ▸

Hunting Percival Jet Provost T.1. ▸

G-AOBU
007

Lockheed C-130 Hercules. ▸

The Red Arrows – also known as
The Royal Air Force Aerobatic Team. ▸

British Aerospace Harrier GR.9. ▸

Hawker Siddeley Harrier GR3 XZ991
'Zero Seven' in No. 1 Sqn markings,
complete with arctic camouflage. ▸

BAE Systems Hawk T1A ▸

Three SEPECAT Jaguars, including a GR3 and a T2. The lower Jaguar is painted bright orange. ▸

A Panavia Tornado GR4 and a F3. ▸

Eurofighter Typhoon. ▸

GN A

RAF Puma Helicopter. ▸

Airbus RAF A400M Atlas. ▸

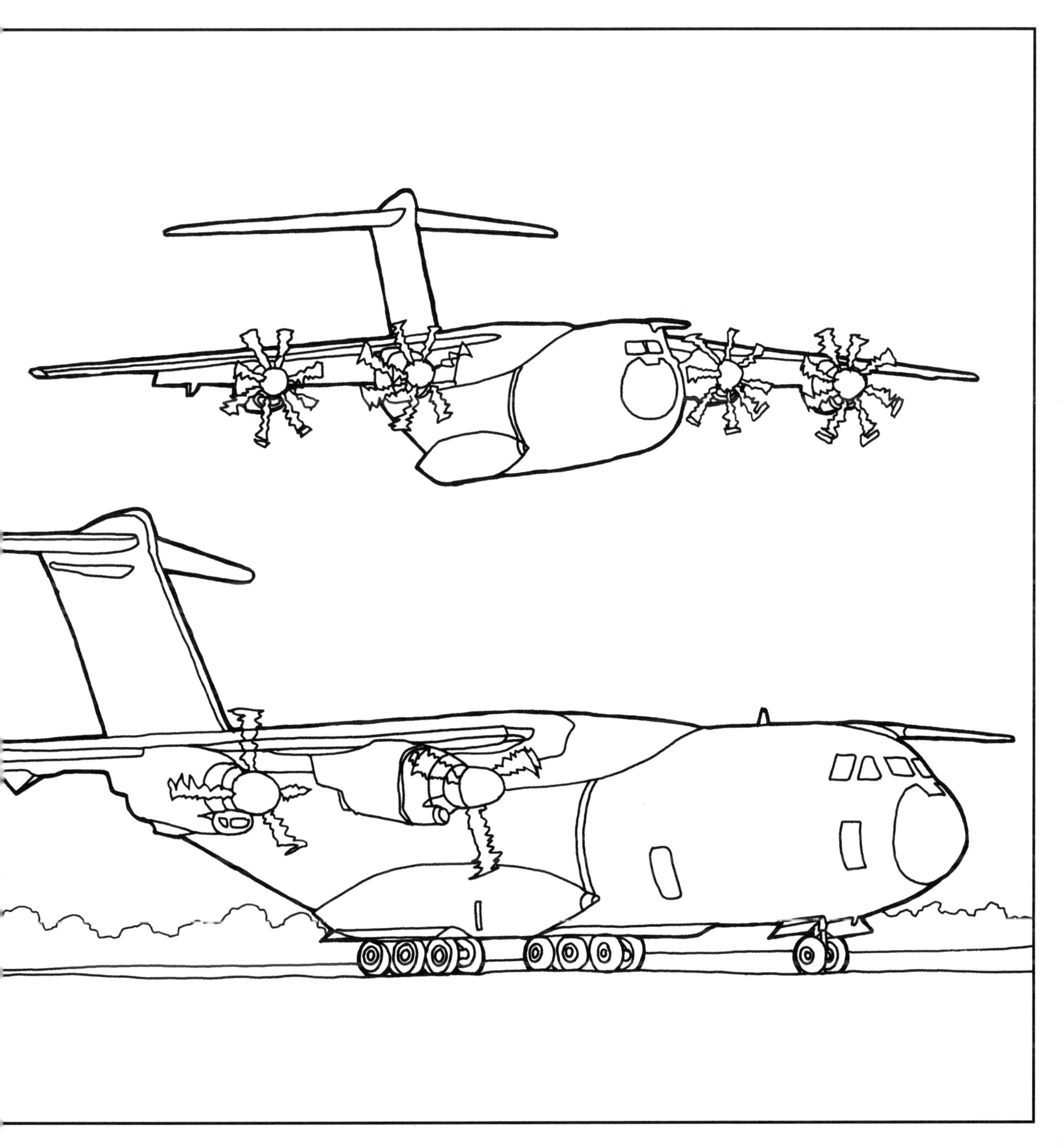

The Red Arrows flying with a Vulcan bomber. ▶

RAF Chinook helicopter. ▸

Lockheed Martin F-35 Lightning II. ▸

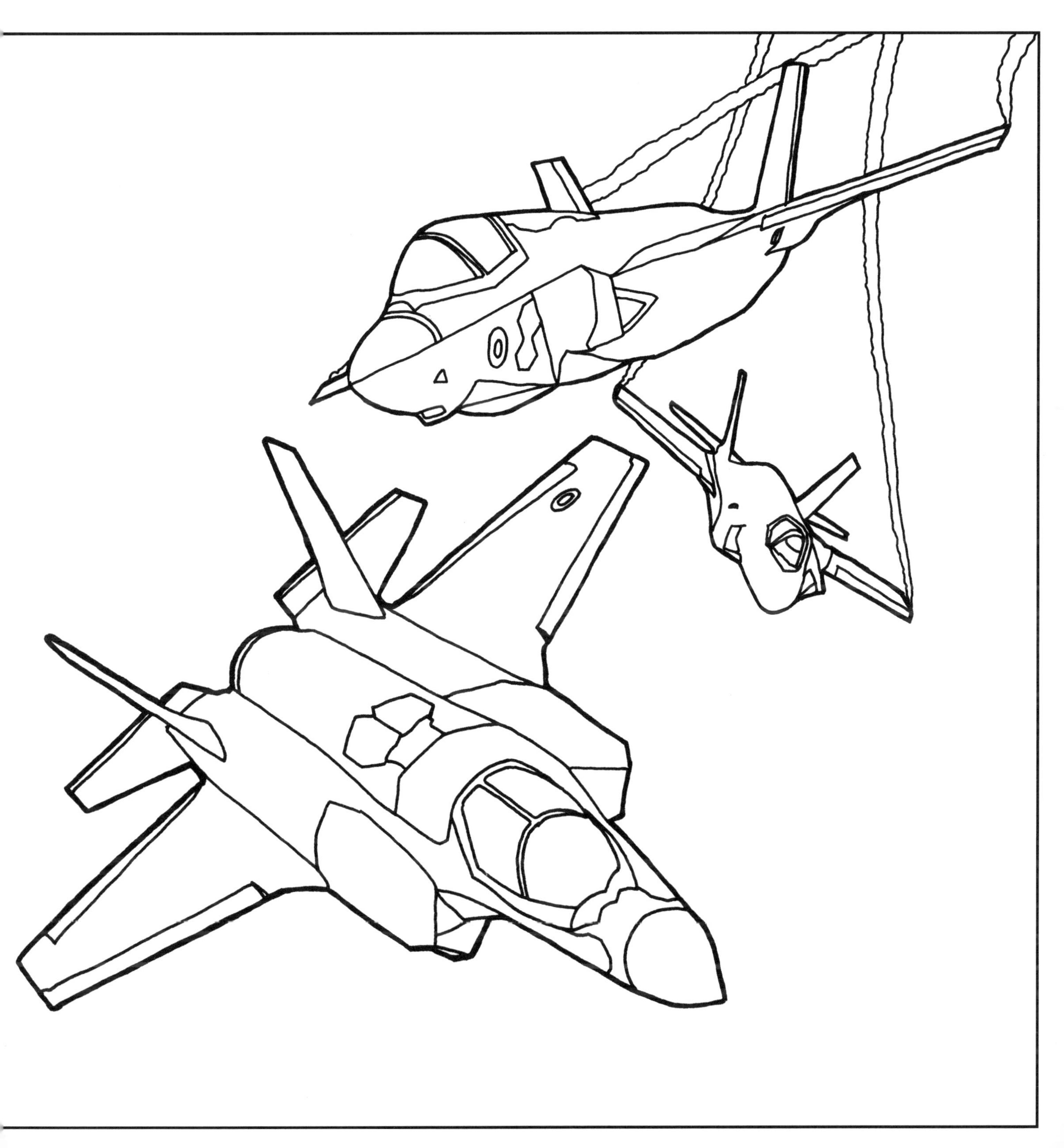

RAF uniforms through time. ▸

ANDI V COLL
RAF REGIMENT

Credits

All artwork created by Martin Latham.

Original scenes created by Martin Latham:
Sopwith Camel; Battle of Britain - Heinkel, Messerschmitt, Hurricane; Hurricane, Spitfire, Lancaster: Stalwarts of the Skies; Battle of Britain – Spitfires and Stukas; Wellington Bombers; Operation Chastise – The Dams Raid

Selected artwork inspired by:

Tiger Moth Ad Meskens
Gloster Gladiator I Alan Wilson, CC 2.0 (lower)
Halifax Bomber photograph from the collections of the State Library of NSW
Hurricanes, Spitfires, Lancaster Ronnie Macdonald, CC 2.0 (upper); SAC Graham Taylor /MOD OGL v1.0 (lower)
Spitfire with Mitchell WyrdLight.com, CC 2.5
Supermarine Spitfire Chowells and Fir0002, CC 2.5 (upper); Seán Pòl Ó Creachmhaoil, CC 4.0 (lower)
Avro Anson RuthAS, CC 3.0 (upper); aeroprints.com, CC 2.0 (lower)
Avro Lancaster Geoff Acton, CC 2.0 (upper), Per from Thunder Bay, Canada CC 2.0 (lower)
Spitfire in flight Tomas Picka/Shutterstock.com
Hawker Hurricane Ronnie Macdonald, CC 2.0
Hawker Typhoon The Flight archive from Flightglobal, CC 4.0
Gloster Whittle Hugh Llewelyn, CC 2.0 (lower); Alan Wilson, CC 2.0 (upper)
Gloster Meteor Roland Turner, CC 2.0 (lower)
DH-106 Comet Ralf Manteufel (upper); Stephen Boisvert, CC 2.0 (lower)
Canberra Mike Freer, Touchdown-aviation (lower)
Gloster Javelin Tony Hisgett, CC 2.0 (upper); RuthAS, CC 3.0 (lower)
English Electric/BAC Lightning Mike Freer, Touchdown Aviation (upper); Andrew Thomas, CC 2.0
Hawker Hunter Carlos Menendez San Juan, CC 4.0 (lower)
Jet Provost RuthAS, CC 3.0 (upper); Mike Freer, Touchdown Aviation (lower)
C-130 Hercules Nilfanion, CC 4.0
Red Arrows Cpl Andy Benson/MOD OGL V1.0
BAE Harrier GR9 Dan Davison, CC 2.0 (lower)
Hawker Siddeley Harrier Kev Gregory/Shutterstock.com
BAE Hawk Dan Davidson, CC 2.0 (lower)
Sepecat Jaguar Clemens Vasters, CC 2.0 (lower)
Panavia Tornado SAC Kay-Marie Bingham, RAF/MOD, OGL V1.0 (upper); Carlos Menendez San Juan, CC 2.0 (lower)
Eurofighter Typhoon Mark Harkin, CC 2.0 (lower)
Puma Sgt Jack Pritchard, CC(RAF)/MOD LGL v.1.0 (upper); Cpl Scott Robertson/MOD OGL V1.0 (lower)
A400M Atlas Paul Crouch/MOD, OGL v1.0 (upper); Paul Crouch/MoD, OGL v2.0 (lower)
The Red Arrows flying with a Vulcan bomber. Cpl Steve Buckley RAF/MoD OGL v1.0
RAF Chinook Cpl David Rose/MOD, OGL v1.0 (upper); Dan Marsh, CC 3.0 (lower)
Lightning II SAC Tim Laurence/MOD, OGL v.1.0.
Uniforms SAC Andy Masson OGL v1.0 (right)

All images via Wikimedia Commons